A
FATHER'S
WISDOM

A BOOK OF QUOTATIONS

Creative

ABILITY

"It is not enough to have a good mind; the main thing is to use it well."

(Rene Descartes)

"Natural ability without education has oftener raised men to glory and virtue, than education without natural ability."

(Cicero)

# CHIEVEMENT

"Winning is not a sometime thing; it's an all-time thing. You don't win once in a while, you don't do things right once in a while, you do them right all the time. Winning is a habit. Unfortunately, so is losing."

(Vince Lombardi)

"The harder you work the luckier you get."

(Gary Player)

RGUMENTS

"Arguments are to be avoided; they are always vulgar and often convincing."

(Oscar Wilde: The Importance of Being Earnest, II, 1895)

"When an argument is over, how many weighty reasons does a man recollect which his heat and violence made him utterly forget?"

(Eustace Budgell, The Spectator, 1711)

BUSINESS

"Regardless of what company you work for, never forget the most important product you're selling is yourself."

(Anon)

"Boldness in business, is the first, second, and third thing."

(H.G.Bohn: Handbook of Proverbs, 1855)

"When you dance with your customer let him lead."

(Anon)

CHARACTER

"Every man's character is the arbiter of his fortune."

(Publilius Syrus: Sententiae, c. 50 B.C.)

"When the One Great Scorer comes to write against your name, He marks, not that you won or lost, but how you played the game."

(Grantland Rice)

"Hold yourself responsible for a higher standard than anyone else expects of you. Never excuse yourself."

(Henry Ward Beecher)

# ONFIDENCE

"They can conquer who believe they can."
(John Dryden)

"Some men are just as firmly convinced of what they think as others are of what they know."
(Aristotle: Nicomachean)

"Confidence in an unfaithful man in time of trouble is like a broken tooth, and a foot out of joint."
(Proverbs 25:19)

# CONTENTMENT

"Content makes poor men rich; discontent makes rich men poor."

(Benjamin Franklin: Poor Richard's Almanac, 1749)

"The greatest wealth is to live content with little, for there is never want where the mind is satisfied."

(Lucretius: De rerum natura, V, 57 B.C.)

"I have learned, in whatsoever state I am, therewith to be content."

(Philippians 4:11)

# ONVICTIONS

"Convictions are more dangerous to truth than lies."

(F.W.Nietzsche: Human All-too-Human, I, 1878)

"Convictions are the mainsprings of action, the driving powers of life. What a man lives are his convictions."

(Francis C. Kelley, 1933)

 OURAGE

"Don't be afraid to take big steps. You can't cross a chasm in two small jumps."

(David Lloyd George)

"What matters is not the size of the dog in the fight, but the size of the fight in the dog."

(Coach Bear Bryant)

"Courage is resistance to fear, mastery of fear, not absence of fear."

(Mark Twain)

COVETOUSNESS

"He that loveth silver shall not be satisfied with silver; nor he that loveth abundance with increase."

(Ecclesiastes 5:9)

"Covetousness has for its mother unlawful desire, for its daughter injustice, and for its friend violence."

(Arab Proverb)

"Riches have made more covetous men than covetousness hath made rich men."

(Thomas Fuller: Gnomologia, 1732)

EBT

"Owe no man anything."

(Romans 13:8)

"A man in debt is so far a slave."

(R.W.Emerson: The Conduct of Life, III, 1860)

"Living upon trust is the way to pay double."

(Thomas Fuller: Gnomologia, 1732)

"Debts are like children: the smaller they are the more noise they make."

(Spanish Proverb)

 ECEIT

"Bread of deceit is sweet to a man, but afterwards his mouth shall be filled with gravel."

(Proverbs 20:17)

"Oh, what a tangled web we weave
 When first we practise to deceive!"

(Walter Scott: Marmion, VI, 1808)

"You can fool some of the people all of the time, and all of the people some of the time, but you cannot fool all of the people all the time."

(Ascribed to Abraham Lincoln, c. 1863)

 EEDS

"Let deeds match words."

(Plautus: Pseudolus, I, c. 190 B.C.)

"Our deeds determine us, as much as we determine our deeds."

(George Eliot)

"Deeds are facts, and are forever and ever."

(Thomas B. Reed: 1896)

DESTINY

"Destiny is not a matter of chance, it is a matter of choice; it is not a thing to be waited for, it is a thing to be achieved."

(W.J.Bryan, 1899)

"Thoughts lead on to purposes; purposes go forth in action; actions form habits; habits decide character; and character fixes our destiny."

(Tyron Edwards)

<u>DIFFICULTY</u>

"The best way out of a
difficulty is through it."

(Author unidentified)

"The greater the obstacle,
the more glory we have in
overcoming it; the difficulties
with which we are met are
the maids of honour which
set off virtue."

(Molière)

DILIGENCE

"Without diligence, no prize."
(German Proverb)

"What we hope to do with ease, we must first learn to do with diligence."
(Samuel Johnson)

"The expectations of life depend upon diligence; the mechanic that would perfect his work must first sharpen his tools."
(Confucius)

DRINK

"The priest and the prophet have erred though strong drink ...they err in vision, they stumble in judgement."
(Isaiah 28:7)

"O God, that men should put an enemy in their mouths to steal away their brains!"
(Shakespeare: Othello, II, 1604)

"Bacchus hath drowned more men than Neptune."
(Thomas Fuller, 1732)

# EDUCATION

"An investment in knowledge always pays the best interest."

(Benjamin Franklin)

"Learning without thought is labour lost; thought without learning is perilous."

(Confucius: Analects)

"Give a man a fish and you feed him for one day. Teach a man to fish and you feed him for a lifetime."

(Chinese Proverb)

 NDURANCE

"He conquers who endures."

(Italian Proverb)

"Our strength often increases in proportion to the obstacles imposed upon it."

(Paul de Rapin)

"The greater the difficulty, the more glory in surmounting."

(Epicurus)

ENEMY

"Love your enemies, bless them that curse you,
do good to them that hate you, and pray for them
which despitefully use you, and persecute you."

(Matthew 5:44)

"A man has no worse enemy than himself."

(Cicero: Ad Atticum, X, c. 50 B.C.)

"Though thy enemy seems like a mouse, yet
watch him like a lion."

(Thomas Fuller: Gnomologia, 1732)

RROR

"To make no mistakes is not in the power of man; but from their errors and mistakes the wise and good learn wisdom for the future."

(Plutarch)

"In all science error precedes the truth and it is better it should go first than last."

(Author unidentified)

XCELLENCE

"It's a funny thing about life; if you refuse to
accept anything but the best, you very often get it."

(Sómerset Maugham)

"The quality of a person's life is in direct
proportion to their commitment to excellence,
regardless of their chosen field of endeavour."

(Vince Lombardi)

"Excellence is never an accident."

(Author unidentified)

XPERIENCE

"The reward of suffering is experience."

(Aeschylus: Agamemnon, c. 490 B.C.)

"To most men, experience is like the stern lights of a ship, which illumine only the track it has passed."

(S.T.Coleridge: To Thomas Allsop, c. 1820)

"Experience is of no ethical value; it is simply the name we give our mistakes. It demonstrates that the future will be the same as the past."

(Oscar Wilde: The Picture of Dorian Gray, 1891)

AILURE

"Don't judge those who try and fail. Judge only those who fail to try."

(Author unidentified)

"The man who makes no mistakes does not usually make anything."

(Edward John Phelps: House Of Commons, 1899)

GENIUS

"Genius is 1 per cent inspiration and 99 per cent perspiration."

(Thomas A. Edison, c. 1895)

"When a true genius appears in the world, you may know him by this sign, that the dunces are all in confederacy against him."

(Jonathan Swift: Thoughts on Various Subjects, 1706)

ABIT

"Habit is overcome by habit."

(Thomas À Kempis: Imitation of Christ, I, c.1420)

"For the ordinary business of life an ounce of habit is worth a pound of intellect."

(Thomas B. Reed: 1902)

"We first make our habits, and then our habits make us."

(Author unidentified)

# HESITATION

"No man, having put his hand to the plow, and looking back, is fit for the kingdom of God."

(Luke 9:62)

"While we ponder when to begin it becomes too late to do."

(Quintillian: De institutione oratoria, XII, c. 90)

"And while I at length debate and beat the bush, there shall step in other men and catch the birds."

(John Heywood: Proverbs, 1546)

 MAGINATION

"Man's mind once stretched by a new idea, never regains its original dimension."

(Oliver Wendell Holmes)

"You see things and you say, 'Why?' But I dream things that never were; and I say 'Why not?'"

(Thomas A. Edison)

"Imagination is more important than knowledge."

(Albert Einstein)

# NDUSTRY

"Whatsoever thy hand findeth to do, do it with thy might."

(Ecclesiastes 9:10)

"Sloth makes all things difficult, but industry all things easy."

(Benjamin Franklin)

"The chiefest action for a man of spirit is never to be out of action; the soul was never put into the body to stand still."

(Author unidentified)

JUDGEMENT

"We should be gentle with those who err, not in will, but in judgement."
(Sophocles: c. 450 B.C.)

"Men judge the affairs of other men better than their own."
(Terence, c. 160 B.C.)

"If you judge, investigate. [Si judicas, cognosce.]"
(Seneca, c. 60)

KNOWLEDGE

"Through knowledge shall the just be delivered."

(Proverbs 11:9)

"All that mankind has ever learned is nothing more than a single grain of sand on a beach that reaches to infinity."

(Author unidentified)

"The worlds greatest men have not commonly been great scholars, not its great scholars great men."

(Oliver Wendell Holmes)

LABOUR

"In all labour there is profit."

(Proverbs 14:23)

"The fruits of labour are the sweetest of all pleasures."

(Vauvenargues, 1746)

"Every man shall receive his own reward according to his own labour."

(1 Corinthians 3:8)

LEADERSHIP

"If the blind lead the blind, both shall fall into the ditch."

(Matthew 15:14)

"The manager administers, the leader innovates. The manager maintains, the leader develops. The manager relies on systems, the leader relies on people. The manager counts on controls, the leader counts on trust. The manager does things right, the leader does the right thing."

(Fortune magazine)

# EARNING

"Learning is ever young, even in old age."

(Aeschylus: Agamemnon, c. 490 B.C.)

"A man of learning has riches within him."

(Phaedrus: Fabulae Æsopiae, IV, c. 40)

"Learning is acquired by reading books; but the much more necessary learning, the knowledge of the world, is only to be acquired by reading men, and studying all the various editions of men."

(Lord Chesterfield: Letter to his son, 1752)

LUCK

"I never knew an early-rising, hard-working, prudent man, careful of his earnings, and strictly honest, who complained of bad luck."

(Joseph Addison)

"Good luck is a lazy man's estimate of a worker's success."

(Author unidentified)

 ERCY

"He that hath mercy on the poor, happy is he."

(Proverbs 14:21)

"The mercy of the Lord is from everlasting to everlasting upon them that fear Him."

(Psalms 103:17)

"Nothing is more praiseworthy, nothing more suited to a great and illustrious man than a merciful disposition."

(Cicero: De officiis, I, 78 B.C.)

 ERIT

"The sufficiency of merit is to know that my merit is not sufficient."

(Francis Quarles: Emblems, 1635)

"Nature makes merit, but fortune sets it to work."

(La Rochefoucauld: Maxims 1665)

"It never occurs to fools that merit and good fortune are closely united."

(Johann Wolfgang von Goethe)

ISTAKES

"He who makes no mistakes never makes anything."

(English Proverb)

"No man ever became great or good except through many and great mistakes."

(William Gladstone)

"We learn wisdom from failure much more than success."

(Hugh White)

ONEY

"Better have wisdom behind you than money."

(Ecclesiastes 7:12)

"No servant can be the slave of two masters . . .
You cannot serve God and Money."

(Matthew 6:24)

EIGHBOUR

"Thou shalt love thy neighbour as thyself."

(Leviticus 19:18)

"Better is a neighbour that is near than a brother far off."

(Proverbs 27:10)

"When your neighbour's house is afire your own property is at stake."

(Horace: Epistles, I, c. 5 B.C.)

ORDER

"Have a place for everything and have everything in its place."

(H.G.Bohn: Handbook of Proverbs, 1855)

"Let all things be done decently and in order."

(1 Corinthians 14:40)

"Let all your things have their places; let each part of your business have its time."

(Benjamin Franklin: Autobiography, 1798)

PATRIOTISM

"It is sweet to serve one's country by deeds, and
it is not absurd to serve her by words."

(Sallust: Catiline, c. 40 B.C.)

"Next to the love of God, the love of country is
the best preventive of crime. He who is proud of
his country will be particularly cautious not to do
anything which is calculated to disgrace it."

(George Borrow: The Bible in Spain, IV, 1842)

PEOPLE

"There are three kinds of people in the world, the wills, the won'ts and the can'ts. The first accomplish everything; the second oppose everything; the third fail in everything."

(Eclectic magazine)

"Do not wonder if the common people speak more truly than those above them: they speak more safely."

(Francis Bacon: De augmentis scientiarum, I, 1623)

PERFECTION

"Perfection is attained by slow degrees; it
requires the hand of time."

(Voltaire)

"Be ye therefore perfect, even as your Father
which is in Heaven is perfect."

(Matthew 5:48)

 ERSEVERANCE

"The man who wins may have been counted out
several times, but he didn't hear the referee."

(H.E.Jansen)

"By perseverance the snail reached the Ark."

(C.H.Spurgeon: Salt Cellars, 1889)

"In the confrontation between the stream and the
rock, the stream always wins - not through
strength but by perseverance."

(Author unidentified)

POVERTY

"The needy shall not always be forgotten: the expectation of the poor shall not perish for ever."

(Psalms 9:18)

"Blessed be ye poor: for yours is the kingdom of God."

(Luke 6:20)

"It is not the man who has little, but he who desires more, that is poor."

(Seneca, c. 63)

POWER

"There is no power but from God."

(Romans 13:1)

"Power is precarious."

(Herodotus, c. 430 B.C.)

"To be able to endure odium is the first art to be learned by those who aspire to power."

(Seneca, c. 50)

PRIDE

"When pride commeth, then commeth shame."
(Proverbs 11:2)

"Pride goeth before destruction, and a haughty spirit before a fall."
(Proverbs 16:18)

"Pride breakfasted with plenty, dined with poverty, and supped with infamy."
(Benjamin Franklin, 1758)

QUARREL

"Quarrels would not last long if the fault was only on one side."

(La Rochefoucauld, 1665)

"'Tis by our quarrels that we spoil our prayers."

(Cotton Mather, 1693)

"The second word makes the quarrel."

(Japanese Proverb)

ESPECT

"Respect a man, he will do the more."

(James Howell: Proverbs, 1659)

"To feed men and not to love them is to treat them as if they were barnyard cattle. To love them and not to respect them is to treat them as if they were household pets."

(Mencius: Discourses, c. 300 B.C.)

"Ye shall not respect persons in judgement; but ye shall hear the small as well as the great."

(Deuteronomy 1:17)

RICHES

"He heapeth up riches, and knoweth not who shall gather them."

(Psalms 39:6)

"The quest for riches darkens the sense of right and wrong."

(Antiphanes: Fragment, c. 350 B.C.)

"The rich man is not one who is in possession of much, but one who gives much."

(St. John Chrysostom: Homilies, II, c. 388)

SALVATION

"Strait is the gate, and narrow is the way, which leadeth unto life, and few there be that find it."

(Matthew 7:14)

"Salvation comes from God alone.
[Solo Deo salus]."

(Medieval Latin Proverb)

"Salvation through Christ the Redeemer.
[Salus per Christum redemptorem]."

(Medieval Latin Proverb)

TRENGTH

"Victory does not depend on numbers; strength comes from Heaven alone."

(1 Maccabees 3:19)

"It is excellent
To have a giant's strength, but it is tyrannous
To use it like a giant."

(Shakespeare: Measure for Measure, II, 1604)

"I have strength for anything through him who gives me power."

(Philippians 4:13)

EMPTATION

"Blessed is the man that endureth temptation; for when he is tried, he shall receive the crown of life."

(James 1:12)

"How oft the sight of means to do ill deeds Makes ill deeds done!"

(Shakespeare: King John, IV, c. 1596)

# TOLERATION

"One believeth that he may eat all things: another, who is weak, eateth herbs. Let not him that eateth despise him that eateth not; and let not him which eateth not judge him that eateth."

(Romans 14:2-3)

"It is forbidden to decry other sects; the true believer gives honour to whatever in them is worthy of honour."

(Decree of Asoka, Buddhist emperor of India [264-228 B.C.])

RUTH

"Ye shall know the truth, and the truth shall make you free."

(John 8:32)

"In the end the truth will conquer."

(John Wyclif: To the Duke of Lancaster, 1381)

"Truth is as impossible to be soiled by any outward touch as the sunbeam."

(John Milton: Doctrine and Discipline of Divorce, 1633)

# NITY

"Behold how good and how pleasant it is for brethren to dwell together in unity."

(Psalms 133:1)

"Unity of feelings and affections makes the strongest relationship."

(Publilius Syrus: Sententiae, c. 50 B.C.)

"Unity is the goal toward which mankind moves ceaselessly."

(M.A.Bakunin: Proposition motivée, 1868)

VICTORY

"The race is not to the swift, nor the battle to the strong."

(Ecclesiastes 9:11)

"The object of a good general is not to fight, but to win. He has fought enough if he gains a victory."

(The Duke of Alva, c. 1560)

"It is no doubt a good thing to conquer on the field of battle, but it needs greater wisdom and greater skill to make use of victory."

(Polybius: Histories, X, c. 125 B.C.)

AR

"War is sweet to those who don't know it."

(Desiderius Erasmus: Adagia, 1508)

"All who take the sword die by the sword."

(Matthew 26:52)

"War is the greatest plague that can afflict humanity;
it destroys religion, it destroys states, it destroys
families. Any scourge is preferable to it."

(Martin Luther: Table-Talk, 821, 1569)

# WEALTH

"Many a man has found the acquisition of wealth only a change, not an end of miseries."

(Marcus Seneca The Elder, Letters to Lucillius)

"The poor is hated even by his neighbour: but the rich hath many friends."

(Proverbs 14:20)

"Wealthy people miss one of life's great thrills - making the last car payment."

(Author unidentified)

# WISDOM

"And unto man he said: Behold, the fear of the Lord, that is wisdom; and to depart from evil is understanding."

(Job 28:28)

"Wisdom giveth life to them that have it."

(Ecclesiastes 7:12)

"The wisest man sometimes acts weakly, and the weakest sometimes wisely."

(Lord Chesterfield: Letter to his son, 1748)

YOUTH

"Rejoice, O young man, in thy youth; and let thy heart cheer thee in the days of thy youth, and walk in the ways of thine heart."
(Ecclesiastes 11:9)

"My youth may wear and waste, but it shall never rust."
(William Congreve, 1700)

"Youth is a fire, and the years are a pack of wolves who grow bolder as the fire dies down."
(Author unidentified)

ZEAL

"It is good to be zealously affected always in a good thing."

(Galatians 4:18)

"Zeal without knowledge is sister of folly."

(John Davies, 1611)